365 QUOTES

Daily Quotes to Facilitate a Fulfilled Life

ISBN-13   Paperback   978-1-970309-01-0
            eBook   978-1-970309-00-3

365 QUOTES

Daily Quotes to Facilitate a Fulfilled Life

CECIL G. CLARKE

INTRODUCTION

This book was inspired in a somewhat strange way. There was a certain friend who was always insisting that I needed to hear whatever he had to say. I told him that I did not need to listen to him. All I wanted was peace and quiet. But this would only fall on deaf ears.

I informed him that he was boring and irritating, and that I had no interest in whatever he was saying. But he would continue to speak all the more. I believe he meant well. But I refused to subject myself to listening to someone who just loved to talk. And since I was not getting through to him, I decided that I would do something about it. So whenever he started talking, I would just get up and walk away. Needless to say, I felt bad doing that.

I thought about it and I realize that there are some people who are just like that. And even though they mean no harm, they could really bore you. And so I decided that it would be my own fault if I remained there in the presence of someone who would eventually irritate me. Then it suddenly dawned on me that it could be due to ignorance, or maybe just insensitivity to what affect other people. And I made a resolution that I would be very careful, so that I would never do things like those. And for reinforcement, I decided to put it in writing. And that was the birth of my first four quotes.

The entire contents of this book is based on my own thoughts, and my own experiences. They represent my response, my reaction and my comments in various conversations. They represent my assessment of certain situations. And over a period of about two years I had quite a long list of quotes. And then I became convinced that others could also benefit from them as well. Thus the compilation of this book.

It is my sincere desire that whoever read this book, will find value in it. I have found value in it, and I want to give everyone the opportunity to read it. If they also find value in it, that will make my heart glad, knowing that my effort was not in vain.

I should also tell you that I have a scholarship foundation. Namely:

Suave Scholarship Foundation, Inc.

A certain percentage of the proceeds from the sale of the book, will go toward the scholarship fund.

Thank you so very much, and may God's richest blessings attend all my readers, economically, educationally, socially, and spiritually. May you all be blessed in every aspect of your life.

Email:cecilclarke@msn.com.

Even though you think you know what your
friends need, in reality, you do not know
until you ask them: for they know best.

It is best if the people that are around
you, desire to hear you speak; than
for them to wish that you refrain.

Speech, with all its virtues, can be
boring, as well as irritating: therefore,
you should know when to refrain.

Speak with boldness and clarity, but
know when to refrain. For by so doing,
you will ensure that peace abound.

If you are gullible in this twenty first Century,
that will place you at great peril. For there
are a multitude of information coming your
way daily, most of which are not real.

I need a full explanation from you, but
I will not ask you to put it in words; for
that might be a bit much for you.

Accidents will happen, despite the best
precautions: but without precautions,
there will be much more.

The beauty that glows with radiance when
it is in light, is not altered when it is in
darkness. It is only concealed therein.

There is no limit to what God can
accomplish with a few good men.

Love is a very powerful weapon; but
it does good, and nothing else.

A heart filled with love, has no
capacity for hatred and indifference.
Just kindness and affection.

The greatest joy that a believer can have, is
to know that his or her ways please God.

The greatest preparation that every man
must make, is to meet his Maker. For
ready or not, one day we must all appear
before the judgment seat of Christ.

It is easy for a man to live up to the expectations
of his wife. The difficulty lies in knowing them.

A man needs time to grow up, unless he
knows of a way to skip being a youth.

It is always good to have an opinion, but it
is not always the same when you give it. For
some opinions should be kept to yourself.

Things are not always what you perceive them
to be, therefore you should always get the facts.

A man should always try to be a strong support
for his wife; he should join her in doing good
and noble deeds. Unlike Adam who joined his
wife in disobedience, then try to blame her.

Do not be too quick to form conclusions
about people and judge them, irrespective
of the evidence that you think you
have: for you could be wrong.

There are people who will judge
you by their own standard, and
assassinate you without a knife,
or a gun: they will simply use their tongue.

Be careful how you form opinions about
people and come to conclusions about
them: for you may be embarrassed when
you discover that you were wrong.

Sometimes a man has to be brave enough
to do the good that he knows, even if it is
going to earn him a slap in the face.

Before you start worrying, you should
number and document all the anticipated
accomplishments thereby: and the number
will determine the justification.

From a pessimistic point of view, Adam
lost a rib, but optimistically, he gained
a wife; much to his great delight.

To be a successful liar you will need to
have an impeccable memory: one that
can recall with accuracy, all your lies.

Watching the sunset gives one a most splendid
feeling: for it becomes such a beautiful ray of
light, with the purest grandeur and brilliance,
that touches everything and everyone within
its path; just before dying into the night.

A thing of beauty is a perennial joy. It has the
potential to inspire and influence the hearts
of so many individuals; giving them a positive
and receptive attitude, and transforming
them into productive, and most accomplished
individuals: making tangible contributions

Not every appointment is a prospect; but
every prospect deserves an appointment.

Gladly admit that you do not know it
all, for that is God's prerogative.

There is no better way to help yourself, than
to seek out others in need and help them.

Regardless how difficult a task may
be, it gets easier once it is started.

Everyone should be responsible, but that is not
always the case: therefore, someone must take
the initiative, in order to have some semblance
of stability, and productivity in this society.

Character is determined by what one does when
alone, with multiple opportunities to do good
or evil, and knows that no one is watching.

You are who you are, so pretense or
denial, or anything to the contrary will
not matter: for who you are speaks so
loudly, that nothing else can be heard.

A man may give all that he possessed,
and yet, he has not given all, until he
gives himself. But God gave all.

If a woman is chaste and virtuous, yet
portrays the traits of an harlot: quite likely
she will only be perceived as the latter.

The only way to avoid the look of
disdain from some people, is to
avoid crossing path with them.

Always look for the opportunity to
infect others with your good quality; for
ultimately, the results will be great.

If you have nothing good to say to, or about
someone, it does not conclude that you have
bad to say either. In that case, say nothing!

It is your day off, but that does not give you
licenses to just sit around and do nothing.
That would be most unproductive.

The fact that your expenditure exceeds
your income, does not mean that your
income is not good: for it could mean
that you have over extended yourself.

It is pointless to accumulate an abundance
of material possessions, if you or no one
else is being benefited from them.

Whenever you find that you are inclined to
be sad, you should determine whether you
have the option to do it now, or later. If you
do, then chose later. But for now, be happy.

Whatever is your vocation, be the best
that you can be. But if you are not a
Diplomat, you are not required to be
diplomatic! That is the job of the diplomat!
We all have our own responsibilities.

If you surround yourself with bad
company, there is no way that you can
preserve your own reputation.

If you need more grease to your wheels,
you must let them squeak louder. But by so
doing, you might need more than grease.

If all your opponents are weaklings, you will
never be able to determine your strength.

There are at least two things that are evident at
the end of all competition: A winner, and a loser.

Winning in competitions, is not always an
indication of your strength. Sometimes it is an
indication of the weakness of the opponents.

The wearing of pants is not sufficient proof
that you are a man: women also wear them.

The times of crisis are the times that really
try men's soul. But from these, men can
also learn some meaningful lessons.

If your phone rings regularly, and even at the
most inconvenient times; this could be a clear
indication that you have
creditors. For not only do
they own your person, but
also your dignity; and
they will try to make it known
wherever you are.

When you kneel in prayer to the awesome God,
who is Creator and Ruler of all the universe,
you must also prostrate your heart lowly at
His feet. For He is worthy of reverence.

It is good that you know the price of everything.
But do you know the value of any?

As a leader in a church organization, you
must be observant enough to notice when
there is an administrative struggle within the
organization. It is then up to you to determine
whether to fuse, or defuse the situation.

Never hesitate to throw out your
trash; for there may be others clever
enough to make it their treasure.

A wasted day is one in which you only
sought to enrich yourself; and more
so, at the expense of others.

The pale hand of death knows no
discrimination. It knocks at the door of the
poor and lowly, and also of the rich and
noble; and seldom leaves empty handed.

Be careful of the web that you weave,
while you are practicing deception. For
you may also be entangled therein.

When digging ditch for others, you can
never be sure that you will not fall over in
it. So my rule of thumb is that you let others
dig their own ditch, if they want one.

The mountain may be a great barrier to you,
but to others, it is a great opportunity to climb.

Because of the challenges of life, great effort
is needed; as a result of great effort, many
great tasks have been accomplished.

In order to achieve anything, one must
venture, with, or without guarantee: for
nothing ventured, nothing achieved.

Death, though real, is not something
to embrace; but if everything else
fails, it will cure your disease. But it
will not be an happy occasion.

As long as there are mountains, there
will be opportunities to climb.

Judgment is not your prerogative, but in any
case, it is not prudent to judge a man, based on
what he said he would do; because he reserves
the right to change is mind. Therefore, he
can only be judged, based on what he did.

Men are always attracted to women: but
attraction is no indication that a man
has the woman's interest at heart. For
there is love, infatuation, and lust.

A man may express with all eloquence, his
most noble intentions; but it is only the
acid test of time that will tell them best.

There is Murphy's law, and there is also
the law of prevention. Any wrong that
you can prevent, must be prevented.

The fact that a professional is engaged,
effectively resolving the issues of others, is
no indication that he or she does not have
personal issues. Everyone needs someone.

A pilot should think twice before assisting
a blind passenger who is boarding the
airplane with a Seeing Eye dog. For it is
quite likely that the other passengers will
think that it is the pilot who is blind.

If your name is Jack, you should think twice
before becoming a pilot. You never know when
someone will come on board and say, hi Jack!

When you are down, there is no where else
to go but up. But if you excel to the top,
without honesty, integrity, and humility;
there is nowhere else to go, but down.

To successfully compete in the marketplace,
you must have the best attitude: you must
offer and maintain the best product,
the best service, at the best price.

A man cannot be famous and keep it in
a vacuum. He needs the endorsement
and the acknowledgement of others.

Accepting a worthless offer with
gratitude, is tantamount to naivety.

Never shun the opportunity to hear
other people's story: that way, your
conclusions will be impartial.

Everyone has a story to tell; therefore you
should seize every opportunity to hear them:
they might just make the difference in your life.

Incompetence is more potent than one would
think. It can tarnish your reputation so bad
that no one will ever want to do business
with you again. Therefore you should
strive diligently to acquire competence
at all cost. It will be well worth it.

There is only one way to ensure that people
do not formulate opinions, or come to
conclusions about you, that are inaccurate.
You must tell everyone exactly what they
need to know about you. Your only challenge
is to find out what they need to know.

When everything is crumbling around
you, that is your opportunity to build
something that will not crumble.

The fact that you are consulting with
even the most competent professional,
does not mean that he or she will have all
the answers. So keep an open mind.

It is true that some men can be slick. But if a
man buys his wife flowers and she tells him
that he is just trying to cover his tracks, you
know that the world is gone to the dogs.

There are those who will utilize all of your good
qualities, but will suppress every opportunity
for you to make further advancement.

It is easy to trust God, but men make it hard,
because they want to depend on self.

There is much that I can say on the
subject in question. But with all due
respect, there is nothing more that I
will say; under the circumstances.

One might think that the man sitting on a power lawn mower, should find something else to do, while the lawn is being cut. But if he gets up, at least the mower will come to a crashing stop, and the lawn still not cut.

The activities of the citizens in general, is an indication of the morality of the nation. And it is their morality that shapes their destiny.

If a nation is headed for total collapse, check the morality of the citizens; and most importantly, the leaders.

It is generally established that peer pressure
is a bad thing. But realistically speaking,
one can also be influenced positively, by
the good examples of his or her peers.

People will always talk, but what they say
will not always be factual; but mostly based
on speculation, assumption, and hearsay.

When you are at the bottom, you need not fear
going down. But you have every opportunity
to get to the top. But you must seize the
opportunities, cherish every moment, and
make the effort, in order to advance.

To every negative, there is a positive.
Dwell only on what will work for you.

In time, dark clouds will gather in the life of
the best of men. And if they are not careful,
they will simply give up in despair. But my
word to every man is this: acknowledge your
limitations, and look to God, for He has none.

Discouragement is a prescription of
the devil, to be used on all his victims;
to minimize and kill their hopes, and
shatter their dreams and aspirations.

If you have critical issues, you must be
careful not to let the information get into
the hands of the wrong individuals: for they
can use them to kneed you like doe, until
there is no more circulation left in you.

If you find that your dreams and aspirations
are hard to achieve, praise God, and trust
Him to see you through: for nothing
that is worthwhile, comes easy.

The failure of these giant financial
institutions, is a great reinforcement of a
most significant fact. The fact that there
is only one safe place to lay up treasures:
and that is in the kingdom of heaven.

It is my firm belief that if men would devout
more of their energies and resources, to
the building up of God's kingdom; then
they would realize much more benefits
from their earthly endeavors.

Think twice before becoming a debtor: this
has the potential to rob you of your finances,
your dignity, your privacy, and your sleep.

As a debtor, if you only knew that it would
cost you everything that you possessed,
then I am sure that you would settle
for any of the other alternatives.

If you are contemplating the accumulation of
debt, here is one fact that you should know.
It could be to your great disadvantage.

As a debtor, you offer great empowerment to
the unscrupulous creditors. You offer them a
designation that is less than honorable. That is,
Legal Robbers. But much to your disadvantage.

If you only knew that you had the capacity
to pay out all that money, in interest, late
fees, over the limit fees, etc., etc., etc., then
becoming a debtor would not even be an option.

Many people are terrified of
monsters, whose existence are only
a figment of their imagination.

Human beings are social creatures, and
people should be so disposed that they
do not become paranoid, when someone
is simply attempting to be sociable.

One should strive to avoid obsession, for
it can lead to great disappointment.

You will not be able to meet certain
expectations: because they are unrealistic.

Technically speaking, attorneys never
lose; it is their clients who do. For
win or lose, they will be paid.

Doctors who book ten to fifteen patients
for the same appointment time, should
take a crash course in economics. It will
most certainly help the economy.

If more people would stop to read the hand
writing on the wall, and heed the councils;
it would make a significant difference for
this, and other generations to come.

We are in the middle of a failed economy,
with many financial institutions in serious
trouble; the value of real estate has decline
considerably: therefore, there is no logical basis
for the drastic increase in property taxes.

With careful steps, you can avoid the
pitfalls of the enemy: but hardly will
you survive the snares of a scheming,
hateful, friend, who operates in secret.

To walk in darkness when there is light,
shows that you are foolish and evil.

Evil influences have a compelling force that
must be resisted, with dependence upon God.

If you have only two options, identify the
popular consensus, then chose the other. The
popular one is usually not the right one.

Pride is a disease that first infected Satan
and affected his mind; making him irrational
and unrealistic: he wanted to be like God.

Pride is a fantasy that infect the mind
like a disease, and affect the ability
to think and act rationally.

There are people who will engage you in long
debates, all because they are not receptive
to the councils that are being offered.

There are those who think that God had a
certain standard for them, when they were
young and ignorant. But they expect Him
to have a different standard for them, when
they are grown and educated.

Whenever you are in the company of others,
never let your guards down and assume
that you are not being observed. Watch
your words and actions, for most likely you
are being scrutinized by someone there.

God has prepared a large place for you.
Heaven! The question is, have you prepared
even a small place for Him in your heart?

If you want to increase your inventory, just
give a smile to everyone you meet. You will
be surprised how quickly your heart will be
overflowing with joy and laughter. And your
health and your bank account
will benefit greatly.

When you view the chaotic state of the
world, and consider that it all started with
pride; one should take every precaution, to
avoid being infected with that disease.

Pride does not get enough credit for
disrupting the lives of so many individuals,
by distorting their dreams and aspirations.

There are some things that you should avoid
at all cost; chaos being the first on the list.

Speculation is good, for you can gain a
lot. The only draw back is that you can
lose a lot. Therefore, you should evaluate
your risk tolerance before speculating.

I am not conversant enough to speak on
the subject of gambling, but at least I know
that there are two kinds of people who
should avoid it: those who understand
the pit falls, and those who do not.

Some questions that are asked are not
intended for clarification, or to uncover facts;
but are asked only to provide obstruction,
or to provoke controversy, or to open a
forum so that one can be argumentative.

Even though it may seem that all is lost,
never give up; for if you keep on trying, you
have nothing more to lose: but you might be
pleasantly surprised to see things turn around
in a positive way, with your last effort.

It is great when you have encouragement from
others: but if you don't, all the more reason to
stay focused, and be determined to succeed.

Many great accomplishments would have been aborted, had it not been for the perseverance, determination, and persistence of those who would just not quit, until the goal was achieved.

The fact that the bucket did not reach the water, does not mean that the well is dry: you just need to let down deeper.

The actions of people can be most devastating at times. Nevertheless it is your reaction that is important. For that will determine the make, or break.

If someone addressed you in a derogatory
manner, that does not give you the right to be
embarrassed, or even to feel insulted. First,
you must determine whether that person
even has the capacity to be complimentary.
If not, you need not be phased.

When you borrow or credit, you are not
getting out of debt; you are getting in.

The circumstances of life does not determine
your destiny; you make that determination by
the way that you relate to the circumstances.

Good things do not happen by accident: they
happen by deliberate effort, and determination.

There are people who are preoccupied
with the notion that they are smart. But
it is ironic that when they open their
mouths and try to convince you, they
reflect a totally different picture.

There are people who will
assess you and make the
determination that you are a
bad person. This they
will do without any conclusive
evidence. And you
may protest all you want, but
in their estimation,
you are just the person that
they perceive you to be.

Humor is not always good; for it depends on
the time, and place, and who is present.
For while some will be greatly amused, there
are others who will be greatly annoyed.

Regardless how good and interesting a
story may be, one do not need to hear it
over, and over, and over again. It becomes
boring and annoying, sooner or later.

Because you are so ready to judge
me, even without basis, I must
conclude that you are either a peevish
pessimist, or a diabolical monster.

Your points are not fundamental, yet you
are both argumentatively engaged. My
question is, what do you hope to achieve?

There are times when the most complicated
issues can be simplified, if you talk to the
right person. Your only challenge is to
determine who is the right person.

Every problem has a solution, but panic is not
one of them. Therefore, you should take the
time to find the solution, and do not panic.

Every negative has a positive, and they
serve their purpose, respectively.

The fact that your product and service
is refused, is not always a reflection
of bad quality. Some times it can
simply be a lack of one's ability
to evaluate, and appreciate good quality.

If you should ask me, when is kind gesture
unnecessary? I will simply say, "never!"
And that will be my final answer.

There are expensive women, and there
are also virtuous women. Be careful
not to confuse one with the other.

It is good that you believe and accept the truth
of God's word: but it is best if you obey them.

Some times a man has to be brave enough
to do the good that he knows, even if
that will gain him a slap in the face.

The best time to throw your cigarette away, is
before you smoke it. Any other time, is too late.

Love is the most effective weapon, that
will conquer even the worst enemy.

It is good and commendable that you
are honest. But that does not make you
a hero. For honesty is a given.

Everyone is expected to be honest, but
not everyone is expected to be a hero.

Whenever you have a plan to accomplish
something that you honestly believe is good,
take every step, against all odds, against every
opposition; with full determination to succeed.

Never listen to negative information about
your plan, for that will discourage you
and cause you to abandon your dream.

If you are a member of a committee, or board,
and you are present at all meetings, but never
make at least a verbal contribution, you should
resign, and the sooner, the better. That will
be in the best interest of the organization.

It is the right of all men to excel in their
respective field, or vocational occupation.
But this is not necessarily something that
will be made readily available. So in order to
excel, one must have the determination, and
make the necessary effort, against all odds.

It is a known fact that actions speak louder
than words. But the truth has not been
told about reaction. For it can be the most
devastating, given the circumstance.

There are advisers who will tell you
that what you did was wrong, but only
after the fact. But they can never tell
you what you should have done.

When the word gets around that you are a
generous person, who is willing to help
others who are in a jam; there are those who
quickly formulate in their minds, that, here
is someone that we can shake down. And
they immediately proceed to do just that.

The man who gets accustomed to using
dull cutting tools over the years, places
himself at great risk: For the day he
decides to sharpen them, he could lose
much blood, or even body parts.

There are people who are under the
delusion that they are Christians, but
they possess no such characteristics. They
are neither kind, loving or sympathetic.
Quite frankly, they have no heart.

It is good to have big dreams, but you
must make every effort to achieve
them; at least in some small way.

If you want to be rude and insulting,
you must wait for the right time.
Fortunately, it will never come!

Sometimes you feel that you must speak,
in order to show your brilliance, and be
convincing; but if it causes the prospect
to cancel doing business with you, then it
only prove that the converse is true.

The time is always right to be courteous,
and hospitable, even to a total stranger.

There is great dignity, and nobility in humility.

There is absolutely no dignity
or nobility in hostility.

Discretion is such a great skill, and yet it is
so easy for everyone to learn, and master.

There are certain acknowledgements
that are made at a later date. But all the
indications were there from the very
beginning. People are just not observant.

Discretion has such great intrinsic
value, and yet it cost nothing.

Any group or organization that coldly
take the lives of innocent people, should
bear in mind that it has the potential to
permanently affect the lives of thousands
of family members, and also friends.

Hypocrisy is the fallacy of phony
Christians, plain and simple.

Some people make it their job to see that others
keep the laws: but they give every indication
that they are exempt from keeping them.

We serve a big God, and He has great
plans for the least of us. So let nothing or
no one come between you and Him.

If it is your desire to soar the universe,
then you must let God have His desire
with you: and yours will be most
certainly realized, in due time.

Make God the center of your life, and there
is no limit to the great things that you can
accomplish for His kingdom: For God is
honorable, and He honors faithfulness.

Young man, young woman, if you desire to have
the ideal spouse, in a way, you do have the mind
of God: For that is also His desire from you.

If there is something that you want from God,
ask Him, trust Him, obey Him, serve Him, and
patiently wait on Him: For no good things will
He withhold from those who walk uprightly.

If you are seeking a place of refuge, a
safe place; then you should look for
the best: There is one such place, and
you will find it in the arms of Jesus.

It is no racket science to tell if your ways please
God; for He will magnify Himself in your life,
and give the confirmation of His pleasure.

When standing up against evil, you just have to
stay on your feet: otherwise,
you will get run over.

Evil is no figment of one's imagination. It is
real, and offensive by any standard; and it
has adversely affected the lives of countless
millions, and will continue to do so: until
it is fiercely attacked and destroyed.

Friends are not usually all-purpose; that does
not mean that they are not good: just do
not expect them to be everything to you.

Satisfaction is more likely to be realized,
when one has little, instead of abundance:
for the more one gets, the more he wants.

Sometimes when you are being pursued, it is
only in your best interest: the pursuer is just
trying to warn you of imminent danger.

If God is in pursuit of you, it is only for
good reason. He wants to warn you
of danger, and save you from them;
as you cooperate with His plan.

Some people make it a habit to throw
their obnoxity straight at you, and
yet they pretend that all is well.

Good council should always be sought
and treasured: but the bad ones must
be dispensed with quickly.

Councils come in two forms: good
and bad. So before acting upon them,
do your own due diligence.

You will get many offers to help you,
but some are just ploys to dignify the
curiosity of some inquisitive individuals.

It is impossible to keep peace with all
men. Nevertheless, as far as possible,
you should try; for you may be
pleasantly surprised at the result.

It is hard to accept the idea that some people
are committed to making your life miserable
and impossible. But if and when you do, that
should only strengthen your determination
to be loving and hospitable, while in your
pursuit of happiness and success.

It is very easy to sit around
and wait for others to
take the initiative to make
things happen, so that
you can reap the benefits. But considering that
nothing will happen, if others
should take the same
attitude as you, all the more
reason for you to join
forces with the others, and the
result will be greater.

There are times when you have
exhausted all your energies, and there
is nothing more that you can
do; nothing at all! Now you just feel like you are
ready to collapse in despair and disappointment.
But because you know that you have a God who
loves you; a God who will not quit on you; that
gives you new hope and you
depend on Him: and
in the midst of it all, you found new strength.

There will always be days when everything
that you do, seem to amount to nothing
worthwhile. Those are the days that test your
soul. It is in that test that you determine
whether you are a winner, or a loser.

The fact that it is very easy to lose, does
not mean that it is hard to win. But the
former should provide the motivation, to
make the determination, to do the latter.

There are those who are diametrically opposed
to everything that is logical, good, and ideal.
Therefore, no amount of reasoning,
or negotiation will make a difference
with them. They are
totally set on the destruction of others.

The ignorance and gross misconceptions of
some people, are detrimental to their own
survival and wellbeing, and also that of others.

A man without humility, is a man of stupidity.

It is no racket science to determine that God
is greater than man: it is a universal fact.

Never give up, never become discouraged
by criticism. There will always be those
who feel that it is their bound duty to
criticize, and put down others. It is your
duty to be determined to succeed, to
persevere until your goal is achieved.

If the criticism is not constructive, then it lacks
basis: therefore, it should not phase you.

Many depended totally on the system over
the years: now the system is broken, and
they know of no other way to survive.

Even in the most unstable economy, when
almost all of the previously thriving enterprises
are at the point of total collapse, one can
still find security: but only in the Lord.

With all of the wealth and the abundance of
riches that are in this world; the multimillion
dollar holdings of so many gurus: there is still
no security, except in the kingdom of God.

Always state your truths clearly, but
do not expect to convince all; for you
will be greatly disappointed.

Every once in a while you will be given the
opportunity to positively impact the life of
someone. The choice is yours to determine
whether to trivialize it, or to rise to the occasion
and cease the opportunity to make a difference.

Man, with all his great skills and cunnings,
have achieved some of the most magnificent
accomplishments. There is hardly any limit
to what he can do, except, he will never be
able to find his way to heaven. He can only
get there by faith in, and by surrendering
to the only begotten Son of God.

When you have things to do, it should not
matter what others think, or say; you should
just do them: for you know why, they don't!

If you always wait to get the approval of
others, in order to do what has to be done,
you will always have unfinished business.

If you know that something has to be done,
and you are the one to do it; do not talk about
it, just do it. For there will always be those who
will discourage you, even without basis.

No one operates without an agenda: it
is either yours, or someone else's.

The fact that someone gets on the other
end of your phone, does not mean that you
are going to have a conversation. For there
are people who will keep you there and
talk endlessly: giving you no chance to get
a word in, regardless who made the call.

Not everyone is manipulative, for there
are those with whom you can have a
great conversation on the phone.

There are some things that are quickly relegated
into the background of my consciousness.
Those things can no longer phase me!

Controversy has always been around.
But the ultimate determination is
contingent upon your reaction.

I am not conversant with the intricacy of
the situation, but this one thing I do know;
I have absolutely no interest in being
a party to the matter in question.

Most times when people are
pouting, they confuse one issue with
another. For usually, the one
that they allow to come to the forefront, is not
the one that is responsible for their pouting.

The fact of the matter, the conclusion of the
whole matter, is that there are
people who are hell
bound, and totally committed to the disruption,
and ultimate destruction of anyone who is
unfortunate enough to cross path with them.

It is good if people will motivate and inspire you
to think positively and aspire to do good and
noble deeds. But that should not be the basis
for your motivation. For it is more likely that
they will put you down and discourage you, if
they know that you are giving them the option.

The man or the woman who deliberately
and coldly endangers the lives of others, and
would not even think twice about causing
their death: that person should forfeit all
constitutional rights to due process.

Even the most expensive perfume, will not give
you the smell of purity, if you are not clean.

If you are a positive, enterprising, and
optimistic person, but others think of
you in a negative way; you do not need to
change: they are the ones who need to.

If people are putting you down, and are bent
on your destruction, there is hardly anything
that you can do to change them. So just stay
clear of them, as much as possible, and do
not contribute to any of their schemes.

Be the best that you can be, and keep it that
why, regardless: for there will always be
those who think of you in a negative way.

Wisdom does not come from what is
taught, but from what is learned.

If you nurture your bad, childhood habits, one
day those habits will become grown ups: giving
you the legal age and authority to self-destruct.

Some homes are so nicely furnished
and well decorated; the only thing
lacking is a place to sit.

If you believe that your skills and your brilliant
intellect are too much for you to dedicate to the
building up of God's kingdom, then I strongly
recommend that you give Him your disability
and your limitations. You will be simply amazed
at what He can use them to accomplish.

It is always the right times for going into
business, if you form a partnership with God.

You should try to be flexible when dealing with others. Because they can get pretty complex at times. But at the end of the day, you should try to be yourself. For you are who you are. Otherwise, you could set yourself up as a fraud.

I have in my hand the signed agreement, that you will pay me my money on April 15, 2014. I have only one question for you. When will that be? For today is May 19, 2014.

There are many structures that can be used in running an organization: but the one that is chosen must be carefully followed, to ensure success, and avoid self-destruction.

I have always loved children. But if that
was not the case, I would be quickly
converted by my son and his lovely wife
with their four beautiful children.

Whenever you are able to show kindness to
someone, do not allow any circumstance
to get in the way. Just do it.

If you have interest in something, and there
are many conflicting stories about it; I believe
you should do your own investigation,
before coming to a proper conclusion.

God is omnipotent, omniscient, and
omnipresent. He does not take instructions
from man. But man need to, and must
take instructions from Him.

God is greater than man. He is our
Creator. He knows what is best for man:
He gave instructions that, if followed,
will guarantee man's well being.
Not just for here, but also for the hereafter.

If you drive a mini van, even
if you are not picking
up passengers, you will incur the wrath of the
passenger buss drivers, if you get ahead of them.
They believe you are picking up passengers.

It is most ironic that men are not able to read
your mind, yet they think they know positively
what you are thinking. And based on that they
make decisions that adversely affect you.

You may not always be able to make tangible
material, or financial contributions to your
families; nevertheless, you should not distant
yourself from them. Sometimes, all they need
is to see you, or even to hear from you, and to
know that you are ok, and that you care.

God is the supreme ruler of all mankind, and
He knows how we can best honor Him: and He
communicates this in His holy word. Therefore,
it is folly and a dishonor for man to invent
new ways, according to his own likeness.

God wants man to be happy, but it is
impossible for man to find happiness
by being defiant to Him.

God is the source of knowledge and He made it possible that man may have it endlessly. But the adversary has made inroads into God's plan and has tainted and perverted what was the ideal: and man is left thinking that he is smarter than God.

Man is jumping and railing, like he is the master of his own destiny: but unless he comes to his senses and let go, and let God, he will certainly self-destruct.

It is sad that even though God is so loving and kind and merciful and totally committed to man's salvation; yet many are so defiant and bent on doing their own thing; much to God's displeasure.

Man is claiming ignorance and confusion
about the things of God's kingdom. But for
the most part, that claim is unreal. It is just a
facade, to justify his wilful defiance of God

There are those who will use their office in
God's church, to introduce their own ideas
about worship. They will not be receptive to
any council that they consider to be contrary to
their way of thinking. And so they will engage
you in long debates, just to have their way.

God is not oblivious to the activities
of humanity: but He is patient and
kind; He is longsuffering.
He is not willing that any should perish,
but that all should come to repentance.

It is the believers duty to love and to
devote time, helping others to know and to
understand the things of God's kingdom:
so that they will be able to make informed
decisions about their soul salvation.

Mankind is having a ball, while expressing
disregard for the word of God. But one day
when the time is right according to God's
timetable, He will do His thing. But it will
be a sad day for those who make it their
business to dishonor and defy Him.

It gives me no pleasure, knowing that there are
many who are taking God for granted. And
I often wonder, if there is anything that I am
failing to do, that could have a positive impact
on the life of even one of those people. If so,
I am also guilty of taking God for granted.

If you are a parent, always give positive council
to your children, even if you think that they
are not listening: For when you are old and
fifty, you might be pleasantly surprised to
hear them say, "Daddy," or "Mommy, we
listen to you, much more than you Think."

Some children are bad, but when you have good
children, you should give them credit. For that
will encourage them in their decision making
process, as they face the
challenges of tomorrow.

The people who worship according to their
own standard, think that they are unique
in their theology; and that they can inform
the bible: but I strongly recommend that
they let the bible inform them, so that
they can be in good standing with God.

If you want to keep in good standing with
God, you must learn to keep on your knees
with Him. For therein lies great victories.

You frequently hear people say, "I do not think
that God will do that." Wrong answer! For God
did not leave certain matters
up to man's thinking.
But He is very specific as to what He will do.
So that there will be no misunderstanding.

There are those who think that they can trick
God into doing what they want, even if it does
not please Him. But that is the greatest folly:
For God is smarter and greater than man.

There are times when you have a genuine
situation, yet you are not able to explain it and
be convincing to some people. For they have
preconceived notions about you, that does
not in any way, line up with who you are.

If you are looking for discouragement,
just keep sharing your plans with others.
But if you are looking for success, just
keep working on your plans.

There are people who will accuse you of
making them angry. But that is not the case.
The fact is, they are angry, and you just gave
them the opportunity to be themselves.

If a church leader sets out to usurp the role of a department, and got the support of the board, that could be an indication that God is not leading: and the church could self-destruct.

The bible is God's handbook to man, to guide him in the way of truth and obedience. But some have found an alternative to obedience, and they no longer need God's handbook.

There are many in the church with much talk, but at the end of the day, they sit very low on matters of principle.

A man is not ready to die, until his life is in obedience to the word of God. But there is just one problem. Ready or not, he could die anytime.

The organizations that fail to follow their
own rules, set themselves up for failure.

To do something different, when there
is an established, and required order
to follow, constitute one of the things:
defiance, manipulation, or sabotage.

You should not depend on anyone, unless
you are teaming together to take positive
actions. Even then, you should be prepared
to use your own initiative, just in case your
partner fails to fulfill his end of the deal.

Now that man has failed you, there is just
one option left. And that is to trust God,
which should be your first anyway.

In a metaphorical sense, if you use fraudulent
means to obtain riches, you should keep in
mind that one day you may need it all, to
pay for the treatment of your leprosy.

Be careful that your love for money,
and material possessions, does not
cause you to get leprosy.

If you want to work on the Sabbath, you
should consider becoming a pastor: but you
must always walk in righteousness. The
question is, how will you do that, when
you already have the wrong motive?

Some opportunities are better missed,
than ceased; for they could cause you
great misery, and endless loss.

Every experience has one of two
impacts: either positive, or negative.

A deceiver is also an inventor: he invents
lies, or evidences to deceive his victims.

There are questions that do not require a verbal
answer. Those are the ones you just ponder.

There are many so-called believers, who will not
see heaven. And that is for the simple reason
that they are nothing but conniving phonies,
in spite of their profession to the contrary.

Be careful not to covet the blessings of
others, for you may also inherit their curse.

There is no doubt that we are in a terrible
economic crisis; nevertheless, there is much
that we can all do to help each other. We
can become more positive, and creative; we
can pool our resources; we can share a word
of encouragement; we can share ideas.

There is so much that we can accomplish,
even in this terrible economy; if we come
together and work together wholeheartedly:
with a strong determination to succeed.

In these very difficult times, there is one way
that you can succeed. That is to look around
and identify people with similar interests and
ambitions, and also a strong determination
to succeed: then team up with them and
encourage them and motivate them and help
them: and together, you will succeed.

Some times when a man is bragging
in the presence of his wife, if he could
only read her mind, that would stop him
in his track. For he would know how
much she detests him for doing so.

A man who likes to brag and show off, should
really get the opinion of his wife, at a time
when she is disposed to telling him the truth.

A woman can be the most sincere, when
telling a man that he is no good.

Certain goals can only be achieved, by
pursuing them diligently, but secretly.

There are greater accomplishments in
team efforts, than working alone.

Some times cooperating together on
certain projects, can be more rewarding,
than competing against each other.

Some people think that success
comes by getting
things in their hands, so that they have the
control. But o no! Not so! For success comes by
working at things diligently, and relentlessly.

Any evil ideas that you cherish, must be
relegate into the background of your
consciousness, before they are executed. That
will make you a great asset to the society.

The best way to execute evil plans, is to
suspend them, until they are forgotten.

If you have the compulsion to hurt someone,
you should at least wait until the person is out
of your reach, and is at a place of complete
safety, then you can forget about it.

The next time you decide to
hurt someone, please
talk with me about it: I promise
that I will talk you
out of it, and then you can
always blame me for not
allowing you to do it. That's
what friends are for.

Even if you do not know God, He is still your
Father. For there is only one God who is Creator,
and He is the Father of all mankind. But if you
know Him, you will honor and obey Him.

The man who is not receptive to God, who is the
giver of all true wisdom, will most likely remain
ignorant, concerning the things of His kingdom:
and will continue to embrace
the argument of fools.

If you have the opportunity to be a mirror to
the world, what will they see in you? Will it be
an example that will positively impact lives?
Or will it make them the most miserable?

Not all compliments are of substance: it
depends on the motive, and sometimes
the capacity of the giver.

In your line of business,
whenever you encounter
a rude, and obnoxious person, do
not allow it to discourage you. Instead, take
comfort in the fact that you are not that person;
and let the experience be an encouragement
to you, in the pursuit of your goal.

A man of great substance may lose
everything, weather through disaster, or
burglary, or even through economic collapse.
And yet his greatest loss comes, when he
gives up, and refuses to try again.

Some of the greatest opportunities exist, in the
worst times of crisis: they are just hard to find.

A man should work hard to ensure that he
is able to meet his financial obligations,
and not be stressed out by them. But if he is
getting calls from prospective clients, at 1:00
am, when he should be in his bed sleeping,
then that defeats the whole purpose.

Take all compliments in humility, for some are
mere flattery: and that's the food for fools.

It is God's plan to give the saints a working
vacation in heaven for 1,000 years. It just goes to
show how honorable God is towards humanity.

I do not wish to spend eternity in
heaven, for that is not God's plan.
But I want to spend eternity
in the earth made new, for that is His plan.

I am just a small man with a big life,
but I acknowledge that it is a gift
from God, and I am very grateful.

All opportunities are not lost, until you
give up, and refuse to try again.

Regardless how numerous the opportunities
are that present themselves, nothing positive
will happen, unless, and until you cease them.

Even when all odds are against you,
as long as you are prepared and ready
to try again; the prospect is good!

A life lived without enriching the life of at least
one person, is a life lived without meaning.

If you are living your life and you
cannot identify someone that you have
helped, then your living is in vain.

Be receptive to counsel, but make intelligent
assessment before accepting them. For there
are people with preconceived notions that
biased their mind, and impair their ability
to be objective about certain issues.

There are people who will speak anything
from their lips, without giving due
consideration to the potential harm
that they can cause to other people.

Keep working on your goal, in spite of much
difficulties; and even great efforts on the part
of others to discourage you: for by quitting, you
close the door to every opportunity for success.

You may have many reasons for not
doing the right thing, but all you
need is one reason to do it.

The past can only be used to relate a point,
but it is of no significance to what you need to
do now; in order to produce positive results.

Time wasted, is time spent on things
that simply do not matter.

In order to achieve your goal, you
must have a plan; a plan that you or
someone else is prepared to work.

In order to have any accomplishment,
you must take action.

If you think that a task is impossible,
however simple it may be; you made
it harder to be accomplished.

Fear is the greatest obstacle to achieving
your goal. And yet fear is usually not real.

The key to success lies somewhere in
the cultivation of a positive attitude.

What you know may be good: but
the best results will come from what
you do with that knowledge.

Both opportunities and disadvantages are
present in our lives. That is positive and
negative. We must chose whether to act
on the positive, or on the negative.

Some where in each experience that
we go through, is a positive lesson that
should be viewed for our learning.

Whatever we do, we should endeavor to do
our best; regardless the compensation.

Opportunities are always there: they just
need to be discovered and ceased.

Success is not something that you receive,
but rather, something that you make.

There is no success in negativity: just failure.

Without positivity, and activity,
there can be no success.

If you are just waiting to see if you will succeed,
it is most likely that you will not: For it should
not be a question of if, but when. And your
positive activity will determine your success.

If you are seriously committed to success,
you will give a deaf ear to all negativity.

Know your own limitations, and operate within
that framework. Do not become a victim of
the negative determinations of others.

The best students are the ones with meek,
teachable spirit; they will gain knowledge.
Those who are proud and arrogant,
chose ignorance for their destiny.

Be resolute in your determination
to be courteous,
and hospitable, regardless.
That way, you will not
be phased by the rudeness, and or ingratitude.

You should always be willing and diligent
about doing your part; for there are
tasks that you can accomplish, which
cannot be replicated by others.

No one truly loves work, but when
consideration is given to the
successful completion of
a task, especially a difficult one; then the
feeling of satisfaction that is experienced,
ultimately inspire love for work.

Success is not a coincident, but rather the
result of planning and taking initiative.

Your attitude plays an integral part
in the achievement of your goals.

Menial jobs are only created by
people with menial attitudes.

You can easily tell a pessimist by his
accomplishments; he has none.

It may be good to sit around and dream;
but it is far better to get up and do
something about it today: not tomorrow.

Entrepreneurs are not made by merely
sitting around dreaming, but rather by
getting up and putting ideas to work.

Never allow your failures to get
in the way of your success.

Even if you are the expert, if you
have the ability to team up with
others, the result will be greater.

If you lack dignity, loyalty, and integrity,
you are not required to be yourself.

It takes wisdom to know what to overlook, so
that you can move forward with your plans.

A goal without a plan, is worthless;
for it calls for no action.

Action is the driving force
behind a goal with a plan.

Whatever your situations, make the best of
them; dwell only on the positives, and endeavor
to make them into something better.

Heroes are only identified after the fact.

To be declared a hero, one must demonstrate
strength, perseverance, and great
determination: combined with the diligent
engagement of the best intents for the
accomplishment of a task, against all odds.

If you have something to say, you may say
it; and even if you have nothing to say, you
may say it. But either ways, it will make
no difference; for my decision is final.

An executive is someone who execute his/her
ability to delegate to others to get the job done.

You can dream all day and all night long, but
unless you wake up and take
action; you will never
be an entrepreneur. For you are just a dreamer.

If you want to increase your motivation,
then you must increase your goals.

Never lose cite of the fact that there is only one
you: therefore you are unique. So using this as a
motivation, make every effort, and take all the
necessary steps to be the best that you can be.

Success is not singular, for it is
accompanied by something by which,
or in which one is successful.

Your goal should not just be to make the
sale, but also to make a living. And wouldn't
it be great if you are able to make a fortune?
Therefore it is important to learn the skill of
selling. That will give you endless possibilities.

Theologically speaking, procrastination
is a tool in the hand of the adversary, to
lead the prospective believer to hell.

A hero is not an extraordinary person,
but one who does extraordinary things:
by overcoming great obstacles, through
great strength and perseverance.

In order to be successful, one must have and
apply the energy and ability to be persistent,
however difficult the task may be.

Success is not just dependent upon
one's ability and his or her activity:
but largely upon God's doing.

When you see someone at the top, do not get
carried away. For they did not start there.

www.ingramcontent.com/pod-product-compliance
Lightning Source LLC
Chambersburg PA
CBHW071202300726
48975CB00004B/1248